Dear Parent:

Do you want to spark your child's creativity? Do you want your child to become a confident writer? Road to Writing can help.

Road to Writing is a unique creative writing program that gives even the youngest writers a chance to express themselves. Featuring five distinct levels, or Miles, the Road to Writing program accompanies children from their first attempts at writing to comfortably writing on their own.

MILE 1

A Creative Start

For children who "write" stories by drawing pictures

• easy picture prompts • familiar subjects • places to draw

MILE 2

Creative Writing With Help

For children who write easy words with help

• detailed picture prompts • places to draw and label

MILE 3

Creative Writing On Your Own

For children who write simple sentences on their own

• basic story starters • popular topics • places to write

MILE 4

First Journals

For children who are comfortable writing short paragraphs

• more complex story starters • space for free writing

MILE 5

Journals

For children who want to try different kinds of writing

• cues for poems, jokes, stories • brainstorming pages

There's no need to hurry through the Miles. Road to Writing is designed without age or grade levels. Children can progress at their own speed, developing confidence and pride in their writing ability along the way.

Road to Writing—"write" from the start!

Look for these
Road to Writing
books

Mile 1

Cool School
Super Me!

Mile 2

Boo!
Road Trip

Mile 3

Monkey Business
Sports Shorts

Tips for Using this Book

- Let your child read each page and write a response—right in the book!

- Don't worry about spelling or penmanship. Just let your child enjoy the experience of capturing ideas on paper.

- Remind your child to write at his or her own pace. There's no rush!

- Encourage your child with plenty of praise.

Pencils, pens, and crayons are all suitable for use in this book. Markers are not recommended.

A GOLDEN BOOK • New York
Golden Books Publishing Company, Inc. New York, New York 10106

ISBN: 0-307-45407-X   A MCMXCIX

MONKEY BUSINESS

by Sarah Albee and

_____

illustrated by
John Manders and

_____

Once upon a time...

(Circle the ones you want in your story.)

a fire-breathing dragon

a mean robot

captured

a beautiful princess

a famous acrobat

and ran off to

a mountaintop.

an amusement park.

Write what happened next.

Then,_____

_____

_____

_____

Later,_____

_____

_____

_____

Finally,_____

_____

_____

_____

The
End

Make up an ad for
skunk perfume.

What is the
perfume called?

_____

What is special about it?

_____

_____

Write a sentence that will make people
want to buy the perfume.

_____

_____

Draw your ad here.

Write a recipe for
a witch's brew.

Ingredients:

_____ _____

_____ _____

 ## Instructions:

Mix together one cup of_____

and three teaspoons of_____.

Boil for_____hours.

Then add a pinch of_____

and two handfuls of_____.

Stir_____times

and serve hot.

Draw a picture of someone BEFORE
drinking the brew.

Draw a picture of someone AFTER
drinking the brew.

Things that worry me:

Things I can do about them:

Invent something.
Draw a picture of it.

What does your invention do?

_____

_____

_____

How does it work?

_____

_____

_____

Who can use it?

_____

_____

_____

Fill in the captions.
Then finish the cartoon.

Draw a picture of a dream you had.

Write about your dream.
Who was in it?

_____

_____

_____

_____

_____

What happened?

_____

_____

_____

_____

A long, long time ago...

(Circle the ones you want in your story.)

I went for a walk in the

mud.   sand.   snow.

I followed some footprints that led to a

cave.   forest.   castle.

Inside I saw

some lost pirates.   a very large dinosaur.

a bear with a headache.

Write what happened next.

Next, _____

_____

_____

_____

Then, _____

_____

_____

_____

At last, _____

_____

_____

_____

"That was the police.
We're surrounded!"

Take a phone message from someone unusual.

TIME: _____

DATE: _____

TO: _____

WHILE YOU WERE OUT

_____ CALLED.

MESSAGE: _____

_____

_____

_____

_____

(Sign your name.)

Draw a picture of the person (or thing) that left the message.

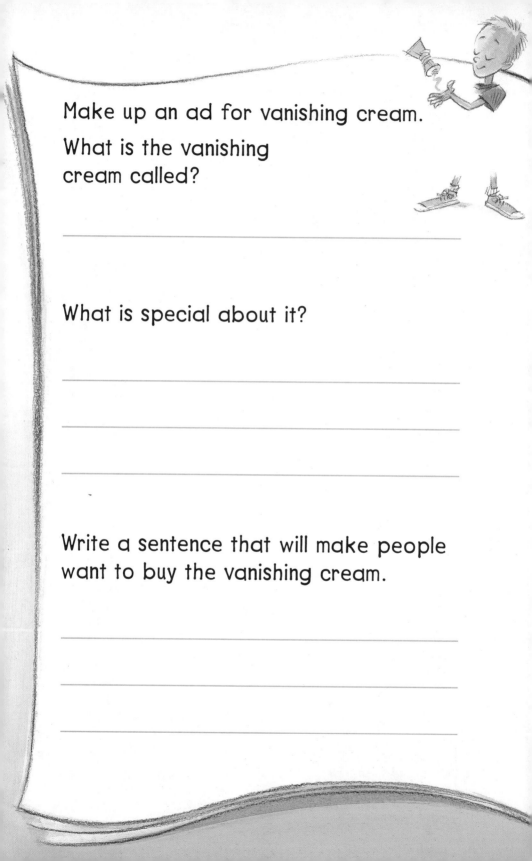

Make up an ad for vanishing cream.
What is the vanishing
cream called?

_____

What is special about it?

_____

_____

_____

Write a sentence that will make people
want to buy the vanishing cream.

_____

_____

_____

Draw your ad here.

Roses are red.
Boxers wear shorts.
I don't want to kiss you
because you have warts.

Write your own poem.

Roses are red.

_____

_____

_____

Draw a picture to illustrate it.

Great Aunt Helga just sent you:
(Circle one.)

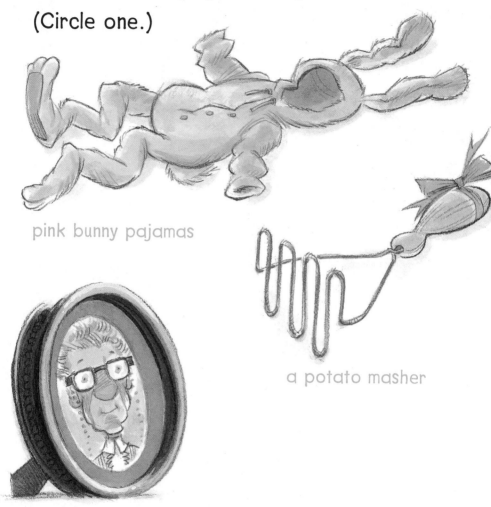

pink bunny pajamas

a potato masher

a framed photo of herself

Write a thank-you note.

Write at least three nice things about the gift.

Dear Aunt Helga,

_____

_____

_____

_____

_____

_____

_____

_____

Love,

_____

A Very Scary Story

It was a dark and stormy night.

"Hey!" cried the kid.

"What's that in my closet?"

Write the rest of the story.

_____

_____

_____

_____

_____

_____

Draw a picture to illustrate it.

Things that bug me:

Things I can do about them:

_____

_____

_____

_____

_____

_____

_____

You just bought something you've always wanted.

Draw a picture of it.

What does it do?

_____

_____

_____

Why did you want it?

_____

_____

_____

Who else will use it?

_____

_____

_____

A VERY TALL TALE

"I just caught a big fish,"
said one kid.
"How big was it?"
asked another kid.

Write the rest of the story.

It was SO BIG_____

_____

_____

_____

_____

_____

_____

_____

Draw a picture to illustrate it.

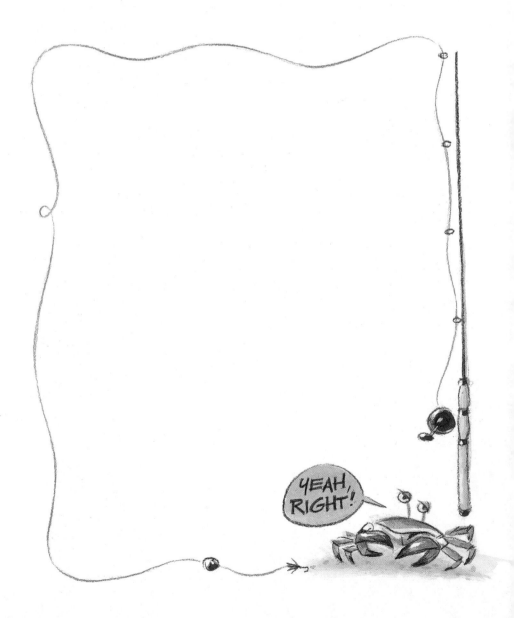

What's the message
in the bottle?

Write a message back.

Write instructions for
catching an elephant.

Step 1:

_____

_____

Step 2:

_____

_____

Step 3:

_____

_____

Step 4:

_____

_____

Draw yourself following one of
the steps.

My Fantasy Room

If you could decorate your room
any way you wanted, what would you
put in it?

_____

_____

_____

_____

_____

_____

_____

_____

Draw a picture of your fantasy room.

Write a recipe for
a mad scientist's
potion.

Ingredients:

_____ _____

_____ _____

Instructions:

Take three _____ .

Mix with one _____ .

Let simmer for_____hours.

Then add a drop of_____

and four drops of_____ .

Shake_____times.

Draw a picture of someone BEFORE drinking the potion.

Draw a picture of someone AFTER drinking the potion.

You're the ruler
of the world!

Nobody is allowed to:

_____

_____

_____

_____

_____

Everybody is allowed to:

_____

_____

_____

_____

_____

Draw a picture of yourself doing something silly.

Write a caption.

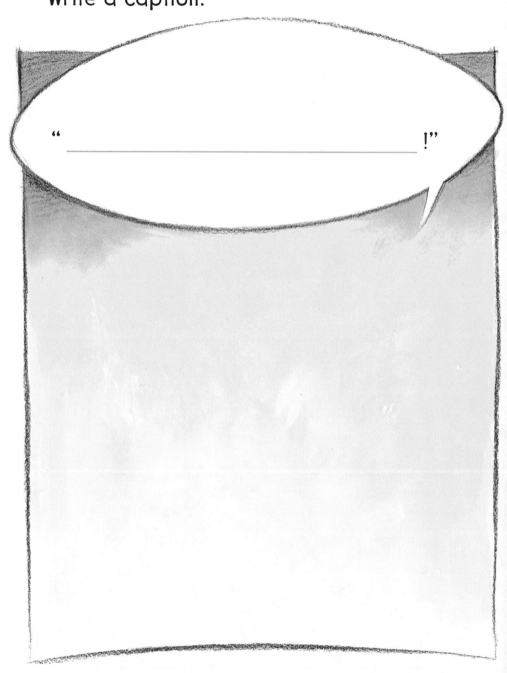

"_____!"